The Mediterranean Diet Cookbook

Dive into 1800 Days of Wholesome Cooking for a Healthier Lifestyle | Easy, Delicious Mediterranean diet recipes for Beginners & Effortless 30-Minute Quick Recipes

Carol Kelley

Table of contents

Introduction

Welcome to the world of the Mediterranean diet—a culinary journey that not only delights the palate but also nourishes the body and soul. In these pages, we'll explore the essence of a lifestyle celebrated for its delicious simplicity, vibrant flavors, and remarkable health benefits.

The Mediterranean diet is not just a way of eating; it's a way of life—one that reflects the cultural heritage and culinary traditions of the Mediterranean region. Originating from the lands surrounding the Mediterranean Sea, this dietary pattern has been cherished for centuries by those who call this bountiful region home.

At its core, the Mediterranean diet emphasizes whole, minimally processed foods, with an abundance of fruits, vegetables, whole grains, legumes, nuts, and seeds. Olive oil, a staple of the Mediterranean pantry, is used liberally, adding a rich flavor and a wealth of health-promoting compounds to dishes.

Fish and seafood feature prominently, providing lean protein and essential omega-3 fatty acids. Poultry, eggs, and dairy are consumed in moderation, while red meat is enjoyed sparingly. Herbs and spices are used generously, infusing dishes with depth and complexity.

The history of the Mediterranean diet is as rich and diverse as the region itself. From the ancient Greeks and Romans to the vibrant cultures of modern-day Italy, Greece, Spain, and beyond, each civilization has left its mark on the culinary landscape, contributing to a tapestry of flavors that continues to inspire and delight.

But the appeal of the Mediterranean diet extends far beyond its delicious offerings. Research has consistently shown that following a Mediterranean-style eating pattern is associated with numerous health benefits. From reducing the risk of heart disease and stroke to improving cognitive function and longevity, the Mediterranean diet has earned its reputation as one of the healthiest in the world.

In this cookbook, you'll find a treasure trove of recipes that embody the principles of the Mediterranean diet, from classic favorites to innovative creations. But beyond just recipes, I'll also share tips and strategies for incorporating the Mediterranean lifestyle into your everyday routine, whether you're cooking for one or feeding a family.

So, join me as we embark on a journey of flavor, health, and vitality—a journey inspired by the timeless wisdom of the Mediterranean diet. Together, let's savor the simple pleasures of good food, good company, and a life well-lived.
Buon appetito!

Chapter 1:

BREAKFAST

Mediterranean Diet Breakfast Tostadas

 4 servings 🕐 15 minutes

 INGREDIENTS

4 corn tostadas

1/2 cup of roasted hummus, red pepper

1/2 cup of diced pepper, red

1/2 cup of chopped onions, green

8 beaten eggs, large

1/2 cup of milk, skim

1/2 tsp of oregano

1/2 tsp of garlic powder

1/4 cup of crumbled feta cheese

1/2 cup of seeded, chopped cucumbers

1/2 cup of diced tomatoes, ripe

 DIRECTIONS

1. In large-sized, non-stick skillet on med. heat, add red peppers.

2. Cook for two to three minutes till they soften.

3. Add milk, eggs, oregano, green onions and garlic powder to skillet while stirring constantly, till egg whites are not translucent anymore, two minutes or so.

4. Top tostadas with hummus, then egg mixture, tomatoes, feta and cucumbers.

5. Serve promptly.

6. If you're actually having trouble getting motivated in the morning, these healthy tostadas will help you out.

7. They're delicious, so the meal won't feel ike a sacrifice.

 NUTRITION

828 calories 48 grams of total fat 471 milligrams of cholestero 1372 milligrams of sodium 49 grams of carbs 12 grams of fiber 12 grams of sugar

Breakfast Recipes Avocado Toast

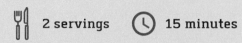 2 servings  15 minutes

INGREDIENTS

1 tablespoon goat's cheese, crumbled

1 avocado, peeled, pitted, and mashed

A pinch of salt and black pepper

2 whole-wheat bread slices, toasted

½ teaspoon lime juice

1 persimmon, thinly sliced

1 fennel bulb, thinly sliced

2 teaspoons honey

2 tablespoons pomegranate seeds

directions

1. Combine the avocado flesh with salt, pepper, lime juice, and the cheese and whisk in a bowl.

2. Spread this mixture onto toasted bread slices, top each slice with the remaining ingredients and serve for breakfast.

3. Serving Suggestion: Serve with scrambled eggs.

4. Variation Tip:Choose perfectly ripe avocados; unripe avocados become hard to mash and aren't flavorful.

NUTRITION

Calories 348 Fat 20.8g Sodium 249mg Carbs 38.7g Fiber 12.3g Sugar 37.4g Protein 7.1g

Raspberry Oats

 1 servings 15 minutes

 INGREDIENTS

½ cup fresh raspberries

¼ teaspoon vanilla

¾ cup unsweetened
almond milk

1 teaspoon honey

2 teaspoon chia seeds

⅓ cup rolled oats

Pinch of salt

 DIRECTIONS

1. Add raspberries into the bowl and mash using the fork.
2. Transfer mash raspberries and remaining ingredients into the glass jar and stir everything well.
3. Cover jar with lid and place in refrigerator for overnight.
4. Serving Suggestion: Add little drizzle of milk and serve.
5. Variation Tip:Add one to two drops of almond extracts.

 NUTRITION

Calories 289 Fat 11.1g Sodium 296mg Carbs 41.8g
Fiber 14.2g Sugar 8.9g Protein 8.5g

Breakfast Quinoa

🍴 4 servings   🕐 26 minutes

 **INGREDIENTS**

1 cup quinoa, rinsed

½ teaspoon nutmeg

1 teaspoon cinnamon

⅓cup flax seeds

½ cup slivered almonds

½ cup dried apricots, chopped

2 cups water

 DIRECTIONS

1. Add quinoa and water in a saucepan and bring to boil over medium heat.

2. Turn heat to low and simmer for 8-12 minutes or until liquid is absorbed.

3. Stir in nutmeg, cinnamon, flax seeds, almonds and apricots and cook for 2-3 minutes.

4. Serving Suggestion: Drizzle with little milk and serve.

5. Variation Tip:If sweetness is desired, add splash of honey.

 NUTRITION

Calories 287 Fat 11.7g Sodium 9mg Carbs 35.2g Fiber 7.8g Sugar 2.5g Protein 10.5g

Egg Breakfast Bowl

 1 servings   15 minutes

 ## INGREDIENTS

2 eggs

1 teaspoon olive oil

½ bell pepper, chopped

½ scallion, chopped

¼ cup Feta cheese,

crumbled

¼ cup olives, pitted

Pepper

Salt

 ## NUTRITION

Calories 325 Fat 25.2g Sodium 992mg
Carbs 9.4g Fiber 2.1g Sugar 5.4g
Protein 17.4g

 ## DIRECTIONS

1. In a bowl, whisk eggs with pepper and salt.
2. Add olives, scallion, bell pepper and cheese and stir well.
3. Heat oil in a pan over medium-high heat.
4. Add egg mixture to the pan and let it cook for 2 minutes, then start scrambling the egg mixture.
5. Stir for 3 minutes more.
6. Serving Suggestion: Garnish with parsley and serve.
7. Variation Tip:You can also use goat cheese instead of feta cheese.

Vegetable Egg Cups

 2 servings   30 minutes

 INGREDIENTS

6 eggs

2.7 ounces goat cheese, crumbled

1 ½ cups spinach, sliced

1 red bell pepper, chopped

¼ cup unsweetened almond milk

Salt

 DIRECTIONS

1. Preheat the oven to 350°F.
2. In a bowl, whisk eggs with milk.
3. Add remaining ingredients and stir well.
4. Pour egg mixture into the greased muffin pan and bake in preheated oven for 20 minutes.
5. Serving Suggestion: Allow to cool completely then serve.
6. Variation Tip: You can also use coconut milk.

 NUTRITION

Calories 76 Fat 5.7g Sodium 68mg Carbs 1.5g
Fiber 0.3g Sugar 1g Protein 5g

Breakfast Chives Frittata

 6 servings 45 minutes

 INGREDIENTS

8 whisked eggs

1 teaspoon red pepper flakes

2 garlic cloves, minced

½ cups goat's cheese, crumbled

2 tablespoons chives, chopped

2 tablespoons dill, chopped

4 tomatoes, diced

1 tablespoon olive oil

Salt and pepper, to taste

 DIRECTIONS

1. Grease a baking pan and preheat the oven to 325°F

2. Mix all the ingredients thoroughly in a large bowl and pour into the prepared pan.

3. Place in the oven and bake until the middle is cooked through, around 30-35 minutes.

4. Remove from the oven and serve.

5. Serving Suggestion: Garnish with fresh chopped cilantro.

6. Variation Tip: For a milder taste, omit the red pepper flakes

 NUTRITION

Calories 149 Fat 10.28g Sodium 210mg Carbs 9.93g Fiber 2.3g Sugar 2g Protein 13.26g

Breakfast Hummus Toast

 2 servings   15 minutes

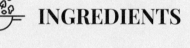

INGREDIENTS

4 slices of rye bread,
toasted

⅓ cup hummus

1 tomato, sliced

¼ cup mixed greens

½ cup red onion, sliced

1 teaspoon each of salt
and pepper

NUTRITION

Calories 148 Fat 4.6g Sodium
261mg Carbs 30.2g Fiber 5.6g
Sugar 3.3g Protein 6.1g

DIRECTIONS

1. Prepare the sliced vegetables while the bread is toasting.

2. Once the bread is toasted, layer with the hummus, tomatoes, onions, and mixed greens to create open-faced sandwiches.

3. Season with salt and pepper to taste.

4. Serving Suggestion: Top with chopped cilantro.

5. Variation Tip: Substitute rye bread with whole-wheat pita bread.

Oat and Berry Parfait

  6 servings   45 minutes

 DIRECTIONS

1. Preheat the oven to 300°F.
2. Spread the oats and walnuts in a single layer on a baking sheet.
3. Toast the oats and nuts just until you begin to smell them cooking, 10 to 12 minutes.
4. Take the sheet out from the oven.
5. In a microwave-safe bowl, heat the honey until it's just warm, about 30 seconds.
6. Add the blueberries and stir to coat.
7. Place one tablespoon of the berries in the bottom of two dessert dishes or 8-ounce glasses.
8. Add a portion of yogurt and then a portion of oats and repeat the layers until the containers are full, ending with the berries.
9. Serve.
10. Serving Suggestion: Garnish with the mint leaves.

 INGREDIENTS

½ cup whole-grain rolled oats

¾ cup walnut pieces

1 teaspoon honey

1 cup fresh blueberries

1½ cups vanilla low-fat Greek yogurt

Fresh mint leaves, for garnish

 NUTRITION

Calories 149 Fat 10.28g Sodium 210mg Carbs 9.93g Fiber 2.3g Sugar 2g Protein 13.26g

Secret Breakfast Sundaes

 4 servings   17 minutes

 DIRECTIONS

1. Preheat your oven to 400 degrees.
2. Arrange your bacon on a non-stick baking sheet.
3. Sprinkle 1/2 of your brown sugar over the bacon Bake for approximately 6 minutes.
4. Turn the bacon and sprinkle the remaining brown sugar over it.
5. Bake for an additional 6 minutes until bacon is dark brown.
6. Remove from your oven and allow cooling on a wire rack.
7. Once your bacon has cooled, crumble it up and set it aside.
8. Beat together with a tbsp maple syrup with a 1/2 cup of cream in a 2-quart metal bowl using an electric mixer.
9. Spoon 2 tbsp of granola into four parfait glasses.
10. Evenly scoop the butter pecan ice cream into glasses and sprinkle them with your remaining granola.
11. Add your coffee ice cream to each glass and evenly drizzle the remaining maple syrup on top.
12. Sprinkle with your bacon and top with strawberries.
13. Serve and Enjoy!

 NUTRITION

Calories: 329 Protein: 7.42 g Fat: 27.55 g
Carbohydrates: 14.41 g

 **INGREDIENTS**

6 slices of Bacon
1/2 cup of Heavy Whipping Cream
5 tbsp of Pure Maple Syrup or Pancake Syrup
3 tbsp of Light Brown Sugar
3/4 cup of Granola Cereal
2 cups of Coffee Ice Cream
2 cups of Butter Pecan Ice Cream
4 Fresh Strawberries

Banana Nut Oatmeal

 1 servings 8 minutes

 INGREDIENTS

Peeled Banana

1/2 cup of Skim Milk

1/4 cup of Quick Cooking Oats

3 tbsp of Honey

2 tbsp of Chopped Walnuts

1 tsp of Flax Seeds

 DIRECTIONS

1. Combine your milk, oats, honey, walnuts, banana, and flax seeds in a microwave safe bowl.
2. Cook in the microwave for 3 minutes, mash your banana using a fork and stir it into the mixture.
3. Serve and Enjoy!

 NUTRITION

Calories: 344 Protein: 6.8 g Fat: 4.09 g Carbohydrates: 75.33 g

---

Greek Frittata Zucchini Tomatoes Feta and Herbs

 4 servings 28 minutes

 INGREDIENTS

6 Eggs

15 ounces of Diced Tomatoes

1 Diced Medium Zucchini

1 tbsp of Olive Oil

2 Cloves of Minced Garlic

1/2 cup of Mozzarella Cheese

1 tbsp of Cream

1/4 cup of Crumbled Feta Cheese

1/4 tsp of Oregano

1/2 tsp of Dried Basil

1 tsp of Spike Seasoning Cracked Black Pepper

 # DIRECTIONS

1. Pour your tomatoes into your colander and allow them to drain out any liquid into your sink.

2. Cut the ends off your zucchini and dice it into smaller pieces.

3. Preheat your broiler.

4. Spray a frying pan with cooking spray heat olive oil in your pan.

5. Add the garlic, zucchini, spike seasoning, and dried herb.

6. Sauté them for approximately 3 minutes.

7. Add your tomatoes and cook an additional 3 to 5 minutes.

8. All the liquid from your tomatoes should be evaporated.

9. While your vegetables are cooking, break your eggs in a bowl and beat them well.

10. Pour your eggs into the pan with your vegetable mix and cook for an additional 2 to 3 minutes.

11. Eggs should just be beginning to set.

12. Add half of your feta and mozzarella cheese.

13. Stir them in gently Cook for approximately 3 minutes.

14. Sprinkle the rest of your feta and mozzarella cheese over the top and allow to cook for three more minutes with a lid covering your pan.

15. Cheese should be mostly melted, and the eggs should be nearly set.

16. Place under your broiler until the top becomes browned slightly.

17. It should only take a few minutes.

18. Keep a close eye on it.

19. Rotate the pan if necessary, to get an even browning.

20. Sprinkle any additional fresh herbs if you so desire.

21. Cut into pie-shaped wedges.

22. Serve and Enjoy!

 # NUTRITION

Calories: 333 Protein: 16.77 g Fat: 26.28 g Carbohydrates: 7.88 g

Chapter 2:
MEAT

Fowl & Feta Fettuccini

  6 servings   🕐 35 minutes

 INGREDIENTS

2-tbsp extra-virgin olive oil

1½-lb chicken breasts, boneless, skinless, and split in half

¼-tsp freshly ground black pepper

1-tsp kosher salt (divided)

2-cups water

2-14.5-oz cans diced tomatoes with basil, garlic, and oregano

1-lb whole-wheat fettuccini pasta

4-oz reduced-fat feta cheese (divided)

Fresh basil leaves, finely chopped (optional)

 NUTRITION

Calories: 390 Protein: 19 g Fat: 11 g
Carbs: 56 g

 DIRECTIONS

1. Heat the olive oil for 1 minute in your Dutch oven placed over high heat for 1 minute.

2. Add the chicken, and sprinkle over with freshly ground black pepper and half a teaspoon of kosher salt.

3. Cook the chicken for 8 minutes, flipping once.

4. Sprinkle over with the remaining salt after flipping each chicken on its side.

5. Cook further for 5 minutes until the chicken cooks through.

6. Pour in the water, and add the tomatoes.

7. Stir in the fettuccini pasta, Cook for 5 minutes, uncovered.

8. Cover the dish, and cook further for 10 minutes.

9. Uncover the dish, and stir the pasta.

10. Add 3-oz. of the feta cheese, and stir again.

11. Cook further for 5 minutes, uncovered.

12. To serve, sprinkle over with the chopped basil and the remaining feta cheese.

Beef Stew

  6 servings   50 minutes

 INGREDIENTS

16-ounces of tenderloin
cut
1 piece of chopped onion
3 Yukon gold potatoes,
chopped up
1 zucchini, chopped
1 cup carrots, chopped
2 cups beef broth
2 teaspoon of sea salt
1 piece of bay leaf
1 tablespoon tomato paste
1 teaspoon onion powder
1 teaspoon paprika
1 teaspoon pepper
2 tablespoons arrowroot
flour
Worcestershire sauce

 NUTRITION

Calories: 310 Total Fat: 8g Carbs: 18g
Protein: 39g

 DIRECTIONS

1. Set your slowcooker to the sautė mode, add the oil and heat it.
2. Add the tenderloin in the oil.
3. Saute them until the meat is well cooked and no longer pink.
4. Add the vegetables and stir in the broth, with seasoning.
5. Close and secure the lid, set to STEW/MEAT mode, with a cook time of 35-minutes.
6. Once cook time is completed, release the pressure naturally for 10-minutes.
7. Ladle ¼ of the liquid into a bowl and mix arrowroot flour with it, making a slurry.
8. Add the slurry back into the pot and stir.
9. Season a bit with salt, serve hot and enjoy!

Pork and Chickpea Stew

 4 servings   8 h 20 min

 INGREDIENTS

2 tablespoons white flour

½ cup chicken stock

1 tablespoon ginger, grated

1 teaspoon coriander, ground

2 teaspoons cumin, ground

Salt and black pepper to taste

2 and ½ pounds pork butt, cubed

28 ounces canned tomatoes, drained and chopped

4 ounces carrots, chopped

1 red onion cut in wedges

4 garlic cloves, minced

½ cup apricots, cut in quarters

1 cup couscous, cooked

15 ounces canned chickpeas, drained

Cilantro, chopped for serving

 DIRECTIONS

1. Put stock in your slow cooker. Add flour, cumin, ginger, coriander, salt and pepper, and stir.

2. Add tomatoes, pork, carrots, garlic, onion, and apricots, cover the cooker and cook on Low for 7 hours and 50 minutes.

3. Add chickpeas and couscous, cover and cook for 10 more minutes. Divide on plates, sprinkle cilantro and serve right away.

 NUTRITION

Calories 76 Fat 5.7g Sodium 68mg Carbs 1.5g Fiber 0.3g Sugar 1g Protein 5g

INGREDIENTS

2 pounds pork neck

1 tablespoon white flour

1 and ½ tablespoons olive oil

2 eggplants, chopped

1 brown onion, chopped

1 red bell pepper, chopped

3 garlic cloves, minced

1 tablespoon thyme, dried

2 teaspoons sage, dried

4 ounces canned white beans, drained

1 cup chicken stock

12 ounces zucchinis, chopped

Salt and pepper to taste

2 tablespoons tomato paste

NUTRITION

Calories: 310 Protein: 12 g
Fat: 3 g Carbs: 8 g

Pork and Bean Stew

 4 servings   4 h 20 min

DIRECTIONS

1. In a bowl, mix flour with salt, pepper, pork neck and toss.

2. Heat a pan with 2 teaspoons oil over medium-high heat, add pork and cook for 3 minutes on each side.

3. Transfer pork to a slow cooker and leave aside.

4. Heat the remaining oil in the same pan over medium heat, add eggplant, onion, bell pepper, thyme, sage, and garlic, stir and cook for 5 minutes.

5. Add reserved flour, stir and cook for 1 more minute.

6. Add to pork, then add beans, stock, tomato paste, and zucchinis.

7. Cover and cook on High for 4 hours.

8. Uncover, transfer to plates and serve.

Pulled Pork with BBQ Sauce

 8 servings   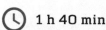 1 h 40 min

 ## DIRECTIONS

1. Add all the seasonings into a bowl to make the spice rub.
2. Cut the roast into 2 pieces.
3. Massage the spice rub over the meat.
4. Place the pork into your pot with the skin side up and pour the chicken stock into the pot.
5. Close and secure the lid to the pot, set to Manual mode on high,with a cook time of 90-minutes.
6. To prepare the BBQ sauce to add all the sauce ingredients in a blender and mix until smooth. Store the sauce in the fridge until the roast is done.
7. Once the cooking time is completed, release the pressure naturally for 15-minutes.
8. Remove the pork from pot and place it on the cutting board.
9. Shred the pork using two forks or tongs.
10. Pour the sauce over the pork and mix it in.
11. Serve warm!

 ## INGREDIENTS

4 lb organic bone-in pork shoulder

2 cups chicken stock

1 tablespoon smoked paprika

1 tablespoon chili powder

1 tablespoon onion powder

1 tablespoon garlic powder

1 tablespoon ground pepper

1 tablespoon of sea salt

½ cup Coconut Aminos

2 teaspoon chili powder

2 teaspoons garlic powder

6 dates, soaked in warm water to soften then drained

¼ cup tomato paste

 ## NUTRITION

Calories: 296 Total Fat: 11 g Carbs: 7 g Protein: 29 g

Yummy Pork Chop

 2 servings  25 minutes

INGREDIENTS

4 pieces of bone-in pork loin or rib chops,
½ inch thick

2 tablespoons clarified butter

½ cup chicken broth

½ cup white grape juice

1 tablespoon of minced fresh dill fronds

16 baby carrots

Salt and black pepper to taste

1 tablespoon of ghee

DIRECTIONS

1. Set your slowcooker to sauté mode. Season pork chop with salt and pepper.
2. Add the chop to the slowcooker and cook for 4- minutes.
3. Cook chops in batches if needed, transferring them to a plate.
4. Add 1 tablespoon of ghee to the pot along with carrots, dill and cook for 1-minute.
5. Add a ½ cup of grape juice and deglaze the pot. Stir in the broth and add in the chops.
6. Shut the lid on the pot, and set to Manual mode, on high with a cook time of 18-minutes.
7. When the cooking time is completed, release the pressure naturally for 10-minutes.
8. Serve by pouring the cooking sauce over the chops.

NUTRITION

Calories: 296 Total Fat: 25g Carbs: 0g Protein: 17g

Artichoke & Lemon Pork Chops

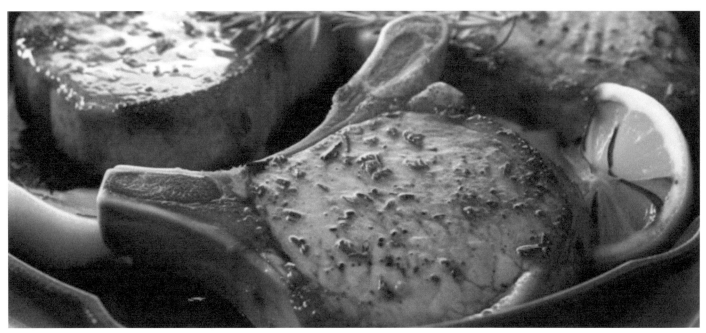

 4 servings   39 minutes

 INGREDIENTS

2 pieces of 2-inch thick, bone-in pork
loin or rib chops

2 tablespoons ghee

3-ounces of pancetta, diced chunks

2 teaspoons ground black pepper

1 medium shallot, minced

4 pieces of 2-inch lemon zest strips

1 teaspoon rosemary, dried

2 teaspoons garlic, minced

1 portion of a 9-ounce box of frozen
artichoke heart quarters

¼ cup chicken broth

½ cup white grape juice

 NUTRITION

Calories: 245 Total Fat: 45g
Carbs: 12g Protein: 48g

 DIRECTIONS

1. Set your slowcooker to the sauté mode, add the pancetta and cook for 5-minutes.

2. Transfer the browned-up pancetta to a plate.

3. Season the pork chops with pepper and transfer them to your pot.

4. Cook the chops for 5-minutes, or until browned, and then remove to a plate.

5. Add the shallots and cook for 1-minute.

6. Add lemon zest, garlic, rosemary, and stir to release a pleasant aroma.

7. Add the chicken broth and artichokes and transfer the pancetta back also.

8. Transfer the chops back into the pot as well.

9. Close and secure the lid to the pot and set to Manual mode, on high for a cook time of 24-minutes.

10. When the cooking time has completed, release the pressure naturally for 10-minutes.

11. Place the chops on a carving board and slice the meat into strips.

12. Divide into serving bowls, and top with cooking sauce from the pot.

Pork Loin Chops with Pears

 4 servings   27 minutes

INGREDIENTS

2 tablespoons ghee

4 pieces of bone-in pork loin or

rib chops,

1/2 -inch thick

½ teaspoon allspice, ground

½ cup unsweetened pear cider

2 large Bosc pears, peeled,

cored and cut into wedges

2 medium-sized yellow onions,

peeled and cut into 8 wedges

Salt and black pepper to taste

Several dashes of hot pepper

NUTRITION

Calories: 318 Total Fat: 19g

Carbs: 4g Protein: 31g

DIRECTIONS

1. First set your pot to the sauté mode, add the ghee and heat it.

2. Toss your pork chops into the pot and cook them for 4-minutes.

3. Cook and brown the chops in batches and set aside on a plate.

4. Add your onions, pears, into your pot and let them cook for 3-minutes or until lightly browned.

5. Add the cider and stir in the allspice and pepper sauce.

6. Set the chops into the sauce.

7. Close and secure the pot lid, set to Manual mode, and cook on high for a cook time of 10-minutes.

8. When the cooking time is completed, release the pressure using quick-release.

9. Serve warm.

Pot Pork Ragu

  4 servings   60 minutes

 ## INGREDIENTS

18-ounce pork tenderloin

Salt and black pepper as needed

1 tablespoon parsley, fresh, chopped, divided

2 pieces of bay leaves

2 sprigs of thyme

1 small-sized jar of roasted red peppers

1 28-ounce can of crushed tomatoes

5 cloves garlic

1 teaspoon olive oil

 ## NUTRITION

Calories: 93 Total Fats: 1.5 g Carbs: 6 g Fiber: 1g

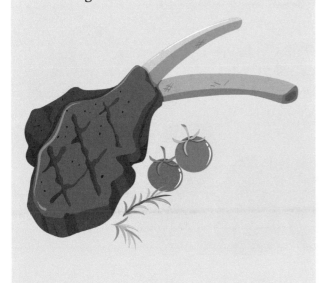

 ## DIRECTIONS

1. Set your pot to the sauté mode, add the ghee to the pot and heat it.
2. Add the garlic to pot and sauté for 1-minute.
3. Remove the garlic with a slotted spoon. Place the pork into the pot and brown for 2-minutes per side.
4. Add the remaining ingredients, make sure to leave half of your parsley for later use.
5. Shut the pot lid and set to Manual mode, on high with a cook time of 45-minutes.
6. When the cooking time is completed, release the pressure naturally over 10 minutes and discard the bay leaves.
7. Remove the pork and shred it and garnish with parsley.
8. Serve warm.

Beef Goulash

 6 servings 30 minutes

INGREDIENTS

2 lbs extra-lean ground beef

2 tablespoons of sweet paprika

1 tablespoon garlic, minced

1 large-sized onion, cut into strips

1 large-sized red bell pepper, stemmed
and seeded, cut into strips

2 teaspoons olive oil

2 cans of petite tomatoes, diced

4 cups beef stock

½ teaspoon hot paprika

NUTRITION

Calories: 283 Total Fat: 13g Carbs: 14g Protein: 30g

DIRECTIONS

1. Set to your sauté mode and add 2 tablespoons olive oil.
2. Add ground beef to the pot and keep cooking and stirring until it breaks.
3. Once the beef is browned, transfer it to another bowl.
4. Slice the stem of the pepper and deseed them. Cut them into strips.
5. Cut the onions into short strips.
6. Add teaspoon olive oil to the pot and add onion and pepper.
7. Add minced garlic, sweet paprika, and cook for 3-minutes.
8. Add beef stock and tomatoes.
9. Add ground beef and close and secure the lid, cook on low pressure for 15-minutes on the SOUP mode.
10. Use the quick-release when cooking is completed.

Korean Beef

 6 servings　　 6 h 20 min

 **INGREDIENTS**

 **DIRECTIONS**

4lbs roast, cut into strips

¼ teaspoon salt

¼ teaspoon black pepper

1 cup chicken broth

4 tablespoons soy sauce

¼ teaspoon garlic paste

¼ teaspoon ginger

1 pear, chopped

2 cups orange juice

1 tablespoon honey

1. Trim extra fat off the roast, rinse and fully dry.

2. Season roast with salt and pepper. Set aside.

3. Set the pot to the sauté mode, add olive oil and heat it.

4. Add the meat to pot and brown on all sides for about 5-minutes.

5. Remove meat from pot and set aside.

6. In the pot pour orange juice, soy sauce, garlic, ginger, pear, and honey and stir to blend.

7. Cover up the pot with the lid and set to Manual mode, on high, for a cook time of 45-minutes.

8. When cook time is completed, release the pressure naturally for 15-minutes.

9. Shred the meat using two forks, then serve with rice and enjoy!

 NUTRITION

Calories: 490 Total Fat: 24g Carbs: 26g Protein: 41g

Rosemary Lamb

 6 servings   50 minutes

INGREDIENTS

4 lbs lamb, cubed, boneless

1 cup sliced carrots

2 tablespoons olive oil

3 tablespoons flour

6 rosemary sprigs

4 garlic cloves, minced

Salt and pepper to taste

1 ½ cups veggie stock

NUTRITION

Calories: 272 Total Fat: 11g Carbs: 9g
Protein: 29g

DIRECTIONS

1. Set your pot to the sautė mode, add the oil and heat.

2. Season the lamb with salt and pepper.

3. Place lamb inside the pot with minced garlic.

4. Cook until the lamb has browned all over.

5. Add the flour and stir, slowly pour in the stock.

6. Add the rosemary and carrots, close and secure the pot lid.

7. Set to Manual mode, on high, with a cook time of 20-minutes.

8. When the cooking time is completed, release the pressure naturally for 10-minutes.

9. Remove the rosemary stems from the pot.

10. Serve lamb with plenty of sauce.

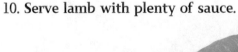

Thyme Lamb

 8 servings   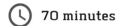 70 minutes

 ## DIRECTIONS

1. Chop the fresh thyme and combine it with the oregano, ground black pepper, paprika, sugar, rice wine, chicken stock, and turmeric, mix well.
2. Sprinkle the lamb with the spice mixture and stir carefully.
3. Transfer the lamb mixture to your pot and add olive oil to the pot.
4. Close the pot and secure the lid, set on MEAT mode for 45-minutes.
5. When the cooking is completed, release the pressure naturally for 10-minutes.
6. Chill the lamb for a little bit before you slice it.
7. Serve warm or cold.

 ## INGREDIENTS

1 cup fresh thyme
2 lbs lamb
1 teaspoon oregano
1 tablespoon olive oil
1 tablespoon turmeric
¼ cup chicken stock
4 tablespoons butter
1 teaspoon sugar
¼ cup of rice wine
1 teaspoon paprika
1 tablespoon ground black pepper

 ## NUTRITION

Calories: 282 Total Fat: 12g Carbs: 8g Protein: 28g

Chapter 3:
VEGETABLE

Ricotta Pizza with Tomatoes and Zucchini

 4 servings  35 minutes

INGREDIENTS

2 cups halved cherry tomatoes

¾ cup part-skim ricotta cheese

2 ½ tablespoons canola oil

2 tablespoons 1% low-fat milk

12 ounces fresh deli whole-wheat pizza dough

½ cup feta cheese, crumbled

2 tablespoons pesto

¼ cup torn fresh basil

1 garlic clove, grated

 DIRECTIONS

1. Place a baking sheet or pizza stone in the oven.
2. Preheat the oven to 500°F.
3. Do not remove pizza stone while the oven preheats.
4. Combine oil and tomatoes on a foil-lined baking sheet.
5. Place it on the pizza stone or shelf above it and bake for 7 minutes.
6. Roll dough into a 13-inch circle on parchment paper; pierce with a fork.
7. Place dough (on paper) on the preheated stone. Bake for 4 minutes.
8. Combine pesto, ricotta, garlic, and milk, and spread over dough, leaving a ½-inch border.
9. Combine zucchini with 1½ teaspoons canola oil. Arrange on pizza, and sprinkle with feta.
10. Bake for 10 minutes.
11. Top with tomatoes and bake another 4 minutes.
12. Top with basil. Cut into 8 slices.

 NUTRITION

Calories: 342 Protein: 15 g Fat: 14 g Carbs: 43 g

Spinach And Lentils Stew

 3 servings   33 minutes

 INGREDIENTS

1 teaspoon olive oil

1/3 cup brown lentils

1 teaspoon ginger, grated

4 garlic cloves, minced

1 green chili pepper, chopped

2 tomatoes, chopped

½ teaspoon turmeric powder

2 potatoes, cubed

A pinch of black pepper

¼ teaspoon cinnamon powder

1 cup low-sodium veggie stock

6 ounces of spinach leaves

 DIRECTIONS

1. Heat a pot with the oil over medium heat, add chili pepper,
2. ginger, and garlic, stir and cook for 3 minutes.
3. Add tomatoes, pepper, cinnamon, turmeric, lentils, potatoes, stock, and spinach, stir and cook for 20 minutes.
4. Divide into bowls and serve.
5. Enjoy!

 NUTRITION

Calories: 220 Protein: 11 g Fat: 3 g Carbs: 16 g

Pea Stew

 4 servings   35 minutes

 INGREDIENTS

1 carrot, cubed

1 yellow onion, chopped

1 and ½ tablespoons olive oil

1 celery stick, chopped

5 garlic cloves, minced

2 cups yellow peas

1 and ½ teaspoons cumin, ground

1 teaspoon sweet paprika

¼ teaspoon chili powder

A pinch of black pepper

¼ teaspoon cinnamon powder

½ cup tomatoes, chopped

Juice of ½ lemon

1-quart low-sodium veggie stock

1 tablespoon chives, chopped

 DIRECTIONS

1. Heat a pot with the oil over medium heat, add carrots, onion, and celery, stir and cook for 5-6 minutes.

2. Add garlic, peas, cumin, paprika, chili powder, pepper, cinnamon, tomatoes, lemon juice, peas, and stock, stir, bring to a simmer, cook over medium heat for 20 minutes, add chives, toss, divide into bowls and serve.

3. Enjoy!

 NUTRITION

Calories: 272 Protein: 9 g Fat: 6 g Carbs: 14 g

Green Beans Stew

 4 servings 35 minutes

 INGREDIENTS

2 tablespoons olive oil

2 carrots, chopped

1 yellow onion, chopped

20 ounces green beans

2 garlic cloves, minced

7 ounces canned tomatoes, chopped

5 cups low-sodium veggie stock

A pinch of black pepper

1 tablespoon parsley, chopped

 DIRECTIONS

1. Heat a pot with the oil, over medium heat, add onion, stir and

2. cook for 5 minutes.

3. Add carrots, green beans, garlic, tomatoes, black pepper and

4. stock, stir, cover and simmer over medium heat for 20 minutes.

5. Add parsley, divide into bowls and serve for lunch.

6. Enjoy!

 NUTRITION

Calories: 281 Protein: 11 g Fat: 5 g Carbs: 14 g

Jackfruit And Chili Stew

 4 servings   35 minutes

 INGREDIENTS

40 ounces canned jackfruit

14 ounces canned red chili puree

1 yellow onion, chopped

8 garlic cloves, minced

1 tablespoon olive oil

6 cups low-sodium veggie stock

1 tablespoon oregano, chopped

1 tablespoon cilantro, chopped

 DIRECTIONS

1. Heat a pot with the oil, over medium-high heat, add onion and garlic, stir and cook for 4-5 minutes.
2. Add jackfruit, chili puree and stock, stir, cover and cook over medium heat for 15 minutes.
3. Add oregano and cilantro, stir, cook for 5 minutes more, divide into bowls and serve.
4. Enjoy!

 NUTRITION

Calories: 263 Protein: 11 g Fat: 6 g Carbs: 13 g

Eggplant Stew

  4 servings   30 minutes

 ## INGREDIENTS

½ teaspoon cumin seeds

1 tablespoon coriander seeds

½ teaspoon mustard seeds

1 tablespoon olive oil

1 tablespoon ginger, grated

2 garlic cloves, minced

1 green chili pepper, chopped

A pinch of cinnamon powder

½ teaspoon cardamom, ground

½ teaspoon turmeric powder

1 teaspoon lime juice

4 baby eggplants, cubed

1 cup low-sodium veggie stock

1 tablespoon cilantro, chopped

DIRECTIONS

1. Heat a pot with the oil over medium-high heat, add cumin, coriander, and mustard seeds, stir and cook them for 5 minutes.
2. Add ginger, garlic, chili, cinnamon, cardamom, and turmeric, stir and cook for 5 minutes more.
3. Add lime juice, eggplants, and stock, stir, cover and cook over medium heat for 15 minutes.
4. Add cilantro, stir, divide into bowls and serve for lunch.
5. Enjoy!

 ## NUTRITION

Calories: 270 Protein: 9 g Fat: 4 g
Carbs: 12 g

Vegetables in a Spicy Curry Sauce

 4 servings 65 minutes

 INGREDIENTS

3 tablespoons olive oil

1 tablespoon curry powder

½ teaspoon cumin seeds

1 eggplant, cubed

3 jalapeno peppers, seeded and minced

4 Yukon Gold potatoes, cubed

3 tomatoes, diced

½ teaspoon salt

½ teaspoon chili powder

½ teaspoon ground turmeric

2 cans (15 ounces each) garbanzo beans or
chickpeas, rinsed and
drained

¼ cup chopped fresh cilantro

Cooking spray

1 tablespoon basil, chopped

 DIRECTIONS

1. In a large pot or Dutch oven over medium heat, heat oil with cumin and curry powder until aromatic.
2. Stir in jalapenos, eggplant, tomatoes, potatoes, salt, turmeric, and chili powder.
3. Cover and cook 30 to 45 minutes, adding water if necessary to maintain a stew-like consistency.
4. Five minutes before ready, add garbanzo beans or chickpeas.
5. Top with cilantro before serving.

 NUTRITION

Calories: 203 Protein: 4.1 g Fat: 8.9 g Carbs: 29.3 g

Breakfast Chives Frittata

 4 servings   35 minutes

 **INGREDIENTS**

4-5 eggplants, peeled and cubed

2 green peppers, chopped

2 red peppers, chopped

1 onion, chopped

2 tomatoes, peeled and grated

2 tablespoons pure tomato sauce

½ cup olive oil

4-5 clove garlic

½ teaspoon salt

1 teaspoon sugar

½ cup dill, chopped

 DIRECTIONS

1. Steep the eggplants in salt water for about 20 minutes.

2. Heat the olive oil in a wide pan and add the onion.

3. After cooking for a few minutes, add drained eggplants, peppers, and garlic cloves.

4. Cover vegetables with tomatoes and tomato sauce.

5. Sprinkle with salt and sugar.

6. Cover the pan and cook on low until eggplants are soft, stirring gently 2-3 times with a wooden spoon.

7. Two minutes before the dish is done, sprinkle with chopped dill and stir.

 NUTRITION

Calories: 406 Protein: 26 g Fat: 31 g Carbs: 5 g

Cauliflower Casserole

 6 servings   45 minutes

INGREDIENTS

1 head cauliflower, separated into florets

1 cup shredded Cheddar cheese

¼ cup finely chopped red bell pepper

1 cup sour cream

¼ cup finely chopped green bell pepper

½ teaspoon paprika

½ cup crushed corn flakes

1 teaspoon salt

¼ cup grated Parmesan cheese

2-3 sprig of parsley or green onion, chopped

NUTRITION

Calories: 169 Protein: 8 g Fat: 13Grams Carbs: 8 g

DIRECTIONS

---

1. Preheat oven to 325°F.

2. Grease a 2-quart baking dish.

3. Place a steamer insert into a saucepan, and fill with water to just below the bottom of the steamer.

4. Cover, and bring the water to a boil over high heat.

5. Add the cauliflower, and steam until crisp-tender, about 5 minutes.

6. Drain and set aside.

7. In a medium bowl, combine Cheddar cheese, sour cream, bell peppers, corn flakes, and salt.

8. Stir in the cauliflower, and transfer to the prepared baking dish.

9. Sprinkle paprika and parmesan cheese over the top of the dish.

10. Bake uncovered until heated through, 30-35 minutes.

11. Top with greens if desired.

Peppery Potatoes (Batata Harra)

 4 servings 28 minutes

 ## INGREDIENTS

4-pcs large potatoes, cubed

4-tbsp extra-virgin olive oil (divided)

3-tbsp garlic, minced

½-cup coriander or cilantro, finely chopped

2-tbsp fresh lemon juice

1¾-tbsp paprika

2-tbsp parsley, minced

Salt to taste

 ## DIRECTIONS

 ## NUTRITION

Calories: 316 Protein: 5 g Fat: 14 g Carbs: 45 g

1. Place the potatoes in a microwave-safe dish.
2. Pour over a tablespoon of olive oil.
3. Cover the dish tightly with plastic wrap.
4. Heat the potatoes for seven minutes in your microwave to par cook them.
5. Heat 2 tablespoons of olive oil in a pan placed over medium-low heat.
6. Add the garlic and cover.
7. Cook for 3 minutes or just
8. enough not to burn the garlic.
9. Add the coriander, and cook 2 minutes.
10. Transfer the garlic-coriander sauce in a bowl, and set aside.
11. In the same pan placed over medium heat, heat 1 tablespoon of olive oil.
12. Add the par-cooked potatoes. Do not stir!
13. Cook for 3 minutes until browned, flipping once with a spatula.
14. Continue cooking until browning all the sides.
15. Take out the potatoes and place them on a dish.
16. Pour over the garlic-coriander sauce and lemon juice.
17. Add the paprika, parsley, and salt.
18. Toss gently to coat evenly.

Chapter 4.

SEAFOOD

Cod With Capers Sauce

 4 servings    25 minutes

 ## DIRECTIONS

1. In a bowl, mix mustard with 2 tablespoons olive oil, tarragon, capers and water, whisk well and leave aside.

2. Heat up a pan with 1 teaspoon oil over medium high heat, season fish with salt and pepper to the taste, add to pan and cook for 6 minutes on each side.

3. In a bowl, mix cucumber with onion, lettuce, lemon juice, 2 tablespoons olive oil, salt and pepper to the taste.

4. Take cod off heat, arrange on plates, drizzle mustard sauce you've made and serve with the cucumber salad on the side.

5. Enjoy!

 ## INGREDIENTS

4 medium cod fillets, skinless and boneless

2 tablespoons mustard

1 tablespoon tarragon, chopped

1 tablespoon capers, drained

4 tablespoons olive oil+ 1 teaspoon

Salt and black pepper to the taste

2 cups lettuce leaves, torn

1 small red onion, sliced

1 small cucumber, sliced

2 tablespoons lemon juice

2 tablespoons water

 ## NUTRITION

calories 278, fat 12, fiber 1, carbs 5, protein 28

Mediterranean Shrimp Dip

 6 servings 35 minutes

 ## INGREDIENTS

1 ounces cream cheese, soft

½ pound shrimp, already cooked, peeled, deveined and chopped

1 cup mayonnaise

½ cup mozzarella cheese, shredded

3 garlic cloves, minced

1 tablespoon Worcestershire sauce

¼ teaspoon hot sauce

1 tablespoon lemon juice

Olive oil spray

½ cup scallions, finely sliced

 ## NUTRITION

calories 175, fat 3, fiber 2, carbs 2, protein 3

 ## DIRECTIONS

1. In a bowl, mix cream cheese with mozzarella, mayo, Worcestershire sauce, hot sauce, garlic and lemon juice and whisk well.

2. Add scallions and shrimp, stir again, pour everything into a baking dish which you've sprayed with some olive oil, introduce in the oven at 350 degrees F and bake for 30 minutes.

3. Transfer dip to bowls and serve.

4. Enjoy!

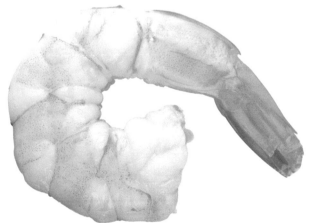

Crab Dip

 10 servings   🕐 40 minutes

INGREDIENTS

½ pound crab meat,
flaked

ounces cream cheese, soft

1 tablespoon dill, chopped

1 teaspoon lemon juice

DIRECTIONS

1. In a bowl, mix crab meat with dill, cream cheese and lemon juice and stir well.
2. Pour this into a baking dish, introduce in the oven at 350 degrees F and bake for 30 minutes.
3. Transfer to a bowl and serve right away.
4. Enjoy!

NUTRITION

alories 321, fat 2, fiber 3, carbs 5, protein 4

Smoked Salmon Dip

 8 servings   65 minutes

 INGREDIENTS

2 ounces goat cheese

4 ounces cream cheese

3 tablespoons beet horseradish, already prepared

1 pound smoked salmon, skinless, boneless and flaked

2 teaspoons lemon zest, grated

2 radishes, chopped

½ cup capers, drained and chopped

1/3 cup red onion, chopped

3 tablespoons chives, chopped

 DIRECTIONS

1. In your food processor, mix cream cheese with horseradish, goat cheese and lemon zest and blend very well.

2. Spread 1/3 salmon on the bottom of a lined spring form pan, press well, add half the cheese mixture and spread evenly.

3. In a bowl, mix onion with radishes, stir and spread over cream mix in the pan.

4. Layer half of the remaining salmon and sprinkle the capers.

5. Spread the rest of the cheese mix and top the rest of the salmon.

6. Cover this and keep in the fridge for 1 hour.

7. Transfer to a plate by removing the ring mold, top dip with chives and serve.

8. Enjoy!

 NUTRITION

calories 254, fat 2, fiber 1, carbs 2, protein 2

Anchovy Dip

 6 servings   15 minutes

 **INGREDIENTS**

8 ounces anchovies in oil, drained

1 tablespoon red wine vinegar

½ cup olive oil

2 garlic cloves, minced

 **DIRECTIONS**

1. In your food processor, mix anchovies with garlic and mix until you obtain a paste.
2. Transfer to a bowl, add olive oil gradually stirring all the time and the vinegar at the end.
3. Stir again well and serve right away!
4. Enjoy!

 **NUTRITION**

Calories: 283 Total Fat: 13g Carbs: 14g Protein: 30g

Special Salmon Tartar

 2 servings 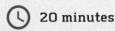 20 minutes

 ## INGREDIENTS

2 tablespoons scallions, chopped
2 tablespoons sweet onion, chopped
1 and ½ teaspoons lime juice
1 tablespoon chives, minced
1 teaspoon sesame oil
1 tablespoon olive oil
2 tablespoons pressed caviar
½ pound salmon, skinless and diced
cherry tomatoes, halved
Salt and black pepper to the taste
12 parsley sprigs

 ## NUTRITION

calories 200, fat 1, fiber 3, carbs 6, protein 6

DIRECTIONS

1. Put the onion in a bowl and mix with scallions, lime juice, chives, sesame oil and 1 tablespoon olive oil and whisk.
2. Roll out caviar, dice it and add to onions mix.
3. Add salt and pepper to the taste and salmon and toss everything to coat.
4. Arrange tartar on serving plates, drizzle some olive oil over them, top with parsley sprigs and cherry tomatoes and serve.
5. Enjoy!

Mediterranean Shrimp

  4 servings   40 minutes

 DIRECTIONS

1. Put 2 garlic cloves in a bowl, add salt and stir very well.
2. Add lemon juice, mayo, cayenne and black pepper and paprika and stir well again.
3. Add 1 tablespoon oil, whisk and leave aside for now.
4. Heat up a pan with the rest of the oil over medium high heat, add onion and fennel, stir and cook for 7 minutes.
5. Add 4 garlic cloves, ground cloves and orange zest, stir and cook 1 minute
6. Add wine, stir and cook for 5 more minutes.
7. Add clam juice, saffron, tomatoes and 1 cup water, bring to a boil, add salt and pepper and simmer for 10 minutes.
8. Add shrimp, stir gently and simmer for 4 more minutes.
9. Discard orange zest, stir gently the whole mix, divide between plates and serve.
10. Enjoy!

 NUTRITION

calories 310, fat 2, fiber 1, carbs 3, protein 4

 INGREDIENTS

1 teaspoon lemon juice

Salt and black pepper to the taste

½ cup mayo

½ teaspoon paprika

A pinch of cayenne pepper

3 tablespoons olive oil

1 fennel bulb, chopped

1 yellow onion, chopped

3 thin strips orange zest

garlic cloves, minced

A pinch of cloves, ground

½ cup dry white wine

1 cup clam juice

1 cup water

1 cup canned tomatoes chopped

1 and ½ pounds big shrimp, peeled and deveined

¼ teaspoon saffron crumbled

Crab Gazpacho

 4 servings 4 h 10 min

 INGREDIENTS

¼ cup basil, chopped

2 pounds tomatoes

5 cups watermelon, cubed

¼ cup red wine vinegar

1/3 cup olive oil

2 garlic cloves, minced

1 zucchini, chopped

Salt and black pepper to the taste

1 cup crabmeat

 DIRECTIONS

1. In your food processor, mix tomatoes with basil, vinegar, 4 cups watermelon, garlic, 1/3 cup oil salt and black pepper to the taste and pulse very well.
2. Pour this into a bowl, cover and keep in the fridge for 4 hours.
3. Divide soup into bowls, top with the rest of the watermelon, zucchini, crab and basil and serve.
4. Enjoy!

 NUTRITION

calories 231, fat 3, fiber 3, carbs 6, protein 6

Wonderful Shrimp

 4 servings   40 minutes

 INGREDIENTS

1 pound shrimp, peeled and deveined

Salt and black pepper to the taste

3 garlic cloves, minced

1 tablespoon olive oil

½ teaspoon oregano, dried

1 yellow onion, chopped

2 cups chicken stock

2 ounces orzo

½ cup water

4 ounces canned tomatoes, chopped

Juice of 1 lemon

¼ cup parmesan, grated

½ cup peas

 DIRECTIONS

1. Put shrimp in a bowl, mix with salt and pepper to the taste and leave aside for now.

2. Heat up a pan with the oil over medium high heat, add onion, garlic and oregano, stir and cook for 4 minutes.

3. Add orzo, stir and cook for 2 more minutes.

4. Add stock and ½ cup water, bring to a boil, cover, reduce heat to low and cook for 12 minutes.

5. Add peas, lemon juice, tomatoes and shrimp and stir gently.

6. Sprinkle parmesan on top, introduce in the oven at 400 degrees F and bake for 14 minutes.

7. Take out of the oven and serve right away.

8. Enjoy!

 NUTRITION   calories 298, fat 4, fiber 3, carbs 7, protein 8

Shrimp Delight

 24 servings 🕐 1 h 26 min

INGREDIENTS

24 medium shrimp, cooked,
peeled and deveined

24 baguette slices, toasted

½ cup raisins

4 cups yellow onion, chopped

2 tablespoons olive oil

2 tablespoons capers, chopped

2 tablespoons dill, chopped

Salt and black pepper to the
taste

 ## DIRECTIONS

1. Place raisins in a bowl, cover with boiling water and leave aside for 30 minutes.

2. Meanwhile, heat up a large pan with the oil over medium high heat, add onions, stir and cook for 10 minutes.

3. Cover the pan and cook for another 10-15 minutes.

4. Drain raisins, chop, add to onions and stir well.

5. Also add capers, salt, pepper and dill, stir and cook for 6 minutes more

6. Transfer this mixture to a bowl and leave aside for 20-30 minutes.

7. Scoop this mixture on each baguette slice, add 1 shrimp on each and serve right away.

8. Enjoy!

 ## NUTRITION

calories 200, fat 2, fiber 2, carbs 6, protein 4

Sardines Appetizer

 12 servings 25 minutes

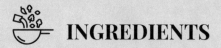 **INGREDIENTS**

4 ounces canned and smoked sardines in olive oil, skinless, boneless and crushed

2 teaspoons olive oil

2 tablespoons mint, chopped

Salt to the taste

slices whole grain baguette

1 small tomato, chopped

1 tablespoon yellow onion, sliced

 **DIRECTIONS**

1. In a bowl, mix sardines with olive oil, salt and mint and stir well.
2. Cut each slice of bread into 4 triangles, place them all on a lined baking sheet, introduce in the oven at 350 degrees F and bake for 15 minutes.
3. Divide tomato pieces on each, add 1 and ½ teaspoons of sardines mixture on and top with onion slices.
4. Enjoy!

 NUTRITION

calories 200, fat 3, fiber 1, carbs 5, protein 5

Chapter 5:
FRUIT & SALAD

Blueberries Stew

 4 servings 20 minutes

 ## INGREDIENTS

2 cups blueberries

3 tablespoons stevia

1 and ½ cups pure apple juice

1 teaspoon vanilla extract

 ## DIRECTIONS

1. In a pan, combine the blueberries with stevia and the other ingredients, bring to a simmer and cook over medium-low heat for 10 minutes.

2. Divide into cups and serve cold.

NUTRITION

Calories 192 Fat 5.4 Fiber 3.4 Carbs 9.4 Protein 4.5

Grapes Stew

 4 servings 20 minutes

 ## DIRECTIONS

1. Heat a pan with the water over medium heat, add the oil, stevia and the rest of the ingredients, toss, simmer for 10 minutes, divide into cups and serve.

 ## INGREDIENTS

2/3 cup stevia

1 tablespoon olive oil

1/3 cup coconut water

1 teaspoon vanilla extract

1 teaspoon lemon zest, grated

2 cup red grapes, halved

 ## NUTRITION

Calories 122 Fat 3.7 Fiber 1.2 Carbs 2.3 Protein 0.4

Mixed Berries Stew

 6 servings  25 minutes

 ## INGREDIENTS

Zest of 1 lemon, grated

Juice of 1 lemon

½ pint blueberries

1-pint strawberries halved

2 cups of water

2 tablespoons stevia

 ## DIRECTIONS

1. In a pan, combine the berries with the water, stevia and the other ingredients, bring to a simmer, cook over medium heat for 15 minutes, divide into bowls and serve cold.

 ## NUTRITION

Calories 172 Fat 7 Fiber 3.4 Carbs 8 Protein 2.3

Lamb & Avocado Salad

 10 servings  60 minutes

 ## INGREDIENTS

1 avocado, pitted

1 cup lettuce

1 tablespoon sesame oil

1 teaspoon basil

1 garlic clove

3 tablespoons olive oil

1 teaspoon chili pepper

1 teaspoon salt

3 cups of water

8-ounces lamb fillet

1 cucumber

 ## DIRECTIONS

1. Place the lamb fillet in the pot and add the water.
2. Sprinkle some salt into the pot.
3. Add peeled garlic clove to the lamb mixture.
4. Close the lid to the pot and cook on MEAT mode for 35-minutes.
5. Chop the avocado and slice the cucumber.
6. Combine these ingredients in a mixing bowl.
7. Roughly chop the lettuce and add it to the mixing bowl.
8. Now, sprinkle the mixture with the chili pepper, basil, olive oil, and sesame oil.
9. When the meat is done cooking—remove it from your pot and chill.
10. Chop the meat roughly and add it to the mixing bowl.
11. Mix up the salad carefully and transfer to a serving bowl.
12. Serve warm.

 ## NUTRITION

Calories: 276m Total Fat: 6g Carbs: 3g Protein: 21g

White Bean and Tuna Salad

  4 servings · 30 minutes

 ## DIRECTIONS

1. Preparing this dish is very easy and can be done even by people who are not trained, cooks.
2. Firstly, you have to put the tuna into a small bowl along with its oil.
3. After that, add the rest of the ingredients, like the beans, onion, capers, olive, watercress, vinegar in the same bowl.
4. Toss it gently and once more after adding salt and pepper to taste.
5. Once done, serve it in a decorated bowl.

 ## NUTRITION

Carbohydrate 20.4 g Protein 22.6 g Fat 4.3 g
Calories: 192.3

 ## INGREDIENTS

2 6-ounce cans tuna packed in oil

1 thinly sliced red onion

3 cups rinsed and drained canned white beans

2 bunches watercress (about 3/4 pound), with the tough stems, removed and leaves chopped (about 2 quarts)

1 tablespoon of drained capers

2 tablespoons of olive oil

1 tablespoon of white or red-wine vinegar

1 teaspoon freshly ground black pepper

3/4 teaspoon salt

Cheesy Caprese Salad Skewers

 10 servings   15 minutes

 INGREDIENTS

8-oz cherry tomatoes, sliced in half
A handful of fresh basil leaves,
rinsed and drained
1-lb fresh mozzarella, cut into bite-
sized slices
Balsamic vinegar
Extra virgin olive oil
Freshly ground black pepper
Toothpicks

 DIRECTIONS

1. Sandwich a folded basil leaf and mozzarella cheese between the halves of tomato onto a toothpick.
2. Drizzle with olive oil and balsamic vinegar each skewer.
3. To serve, sprinkle with freshly ground black pepper.

 NUTRITION

Calories: 94 Protein: 2 g Fat: 4 g Carbs: 15 g

Savory Greek White Fava Bean Salad

  4 servings   🕐 24 hours

 INGREDIENTS

3 Tbsp. olive-oil

1 onion, small and finely chopped Salt

4 ½ Tbsp red wine vinegar

2-3 sage leaves, fresh

3 Tbsp lemon juice, freshly squeezed

Freshly grounded pepper

1 celery stalk, fresh and chopped

1 ¼ cup dried fava beans, white

½ Tbsp of oregano, dried

2 cloves of finely minced garlic.

 DIRECTIONS

1. Beans should be soaked in a lot of water overnight

2. The next morning drain the beans and make sure to rinse it with fresh water.

3. Put drained beans into another pot of freshwater, add sage, cover the pot, and allow it to cook for about 45 minutes.

4. Add salt.

5. Cook for another 15 minutes to allow beans to become soft.

6. Drain the beans, then add lemon juice, olive oil, onion, garlic, oregano, celery, and vinegar. Add pepper to desired taste.

7. Refrigerate for an hour before serving.

 NUTRITION

Calories: 253 kcal Carbs: 28g Fat: 11g Protein: 12g

Bean and Toasted Pita Salad

 4 servings   27 minutes

 ## INGREDIENTS

3 tbsp chopped fresh mint

3 tbsp chopped fresh parsley

1 cup crumbled feta cheese

1 cup sliced romaine lettuce

½ cucumber, peeled and sliced

1 cup diced plum tomatoes

2 cups cooked pinto beans, well-drained and slightly warmed

Pepper to taste

3 tbsp extra virgin olive oil

2 tbsp ground toasted cumin seeds

2 tbsp fresh lemon juice

1/8 tsp salt

2 cloves garlic, peeled

2 6-inch whole-wheat pita bread, cut or torn into bite-sized pieces

 ## DIRECTIONS

1. In a large baking sheet, spread torn pita bread and bake in a preheated 400oF oven for 6 minutes.

2. With the back of a knife, mash garlic and salt until paste-like.

3. Add into a medium bowl.

4. Whisk in ground cumin and lemon juice. In a steady and slow stream, pour oil as you whisk continuously. Season with pepper.

5. In a large salad bowl, mix cucumber, tomatoes, and beans.

6. Pour in dressing, toss to coat well.

7. Add mint, parsley, feta, lettuce, and toasted pita, toss to mix once again and serve.

 ## NUTRITION

Calories per serving: 427 Protein: 17.7g Carbs: 47.3g Fat: 20.4g

Chapter 6:
SOUP

Basil and Tomato Soup

  2 servings · **40 minutes**

 ## INGREDIENTS

Salt and pepper to taste

2 bay leaves

1 ½ cups almond milk, unsweetened

½ tsp raw apple cider vinegar

1/3 cup basil leaves

¼ cup tomato paste

3 cups tomatoes, chopped

1 medium celery stalk, chopped

1 medium carrot, chopped

1 medium garlic clove, minced

½ cup white onion

2 tbsp vegetable broth

 ## DIRECTIONS

1. Heat the vegetable broth in a large saucepan over medium heat.
2. Add the onions and cook for 3 minutes. Add the garlic and cook for another minute.
3. Add the celery and carrots and cook for 1 minute.
4. Mix in the tomatoes and bring to a boil. Simmer for 15 minutes.
5. Add the almond milk, basil and bay leave.
6. Season with salt and pepper to taste.

 ## NUTRITION

Calories per Serving: 213 Carbs: 42.0g
Protein: 6.9g Fat: 3.9g

Cajun Jambalaya Soup

🍴 6 servings   🕐 6 h 25 min

 ## INGREDIENTS

¼ cup Frank's red hot sauce

3 tbsp Cajun seasoning

2 cups okra

½ head of cauliflower

1 pkg spicy Andouille sausages

4 oz chicken, diced

1 lb large shrimps, raw and deveined

2 bay leaves

2 cloves garlic, diced

1 large can organic diced tomatoes

1 large onion, chopped

4 pepper

5 cups chicken stock

 ## DIRECTIONS

1. In a slow cooker, place the bay leaves, red hot sauce, Cajun seasoning, chicken, garlic, onions, and peppers.
2. Set slow cooker on low and cook for 5 ½ hours.
3. Then add sausages cook for 10 minutes.
4. Meanwhile, pulse cauliflower in the food processor to make cauliflower rice.
5. Add cauliflower rice into a slow cooker. Cook for 20 minutes.
6. Serve and enjoy.

 ## NUTRITION

Calories per Serving: 155 Carbs: 13.9g Protein: 17.4g Fat: 3.8g

Cauliflower Soup

 4 servings   60 minutes

 INGREDIENTS

3 pounds cauliflower, florets separated

1 yellow onion, chopped

1 tablespoon coconut oil

Black pepper to the taste

2 garlic cloves, minced

2 carrots, chopped

2 cups beef stock

1 cup of water

½ cup of coconut milk

1 teaspoon olive oil

2 tablespoons parsley, chopped

 DIRECTIONS

1. Heat a pot with the coconut oil over medium-high heat, add carrots, onion, and garlic, stir and cook for 5 minutes.

2. Add cauliflower, water and stock, stir, bring to a boil, cover and cook for 45 minutes.

3. Transfer soup to your blender and pulse well, add coconut milk, pulse well again, ladle into bowls, drizzle the olive oil over the soup, sprinkle parsley and serve for lunch.

4. Enjoy!

 NUTRITION

Calories: 190 Protein: 4 g Fat: 2 g

Purple Potato Soup

 6 servings   🕐 1 h 25 min

INGREDIENTS

6 purple potatoes, chopped

1 cauliflower head, florets separated

Black pepper to the taste

4 garlic cloves, minced

1 yellow onion, chopped

3 tablespoons olive oil

1 tablespoon thyme, chopped

1 leek, chopped

2 shallots, chopped

4 cups chicken stock, low-sodium

DIRECTIONS

1. In a baking dish, mix potatoes with onion, cauliflower, garlic,pepper, thyme and half of the oil, toss to coat, introduce in the oven and bake for 45 minutes at 400 degrees F.

2. Heat a pot with the rest of the oil over medium-high heat, add leeks and shallots, stir and cook for 10 minutes.

3. Add roasted veggies and stock, stir, bring to a boil, cook for 20 minutes, transfer soup to your food processor, blend well, divide into bowls and serve.

4. Enjoy!

NUTRITION

Calories: 200 Protein: 8 g Fat: 8 g Carbs: 15 g

Broccoli Soup

  4 servings   1 h 10 min

 INGREDIENTS

2 pounds broccoli, florets separated
1 yellow onion, chopped
1 tablespoon olive oil
Black pepper to the taste
1 cup celery, chopped
2 carrots, chopped
3 and ½ cups low-sodium chicken stock
1 tablespoon cilantro chopped

 DIRECTIONS

1. Heat a pot with the oil over medium-high heat, add the onion, celery, and carrots, stir and cook for 5 minutes.
2. Add broccoli, black pepper and stock, stir and cook over medium heat for 1 hour.
3. Pulse using an immersion blender, add cilantro, stir the soup again, divide into bowls and serve.
4. Enjoy!

 NUTRITION

Calories: 170 Protein: 9 g Fat: 2 g Carbs: 10 g

Leeks Soup

 6 servings   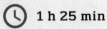 1 h 25 min

 INGREDIENTS

2 gold potatoes, chopped

1 cup cauliflower florets

Black pepper to the taste

5 leeks, chopped

4 garlic cloves, minced

1 yellow onion, chopped

3 tablespoons olive oil

Handful parsley, chopped

4 cups low-sodium
chicken stock

 NUTRITION

Calories: 150 Protein: 8 g Fat: 8 g Carbs: 7 g

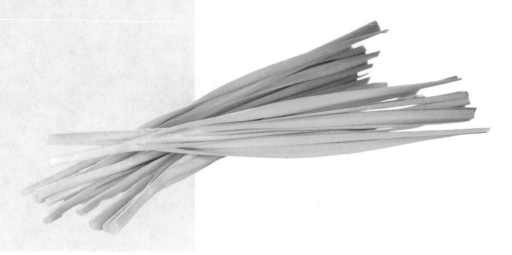

DIRECTIONS

1. Heat a pot with the oil over medium-high heat, add onion and garlic, stir and cook for 5 minutes.
2. Add potatoes, cauliflower, black pepper, leeks, and stock, stir, bring to a simmer, cook over medium heat for 30 minutes, blend using an immersion blender, add parsley, stir, ladle into bowls and serve.
3. Enjoy!

Shrimp Soup

 6 servings   25 minutes

 **INGREDIENTS**

46 ounces low-sodium chicken
stock
3 cups shrimp, peeled and
deveined
A pinch of black pepper
2 tablespoons green onions,
chopped
1 teaspoon dill, chopped

 **DIRECTIONS**

1. Put the stock in a pot, bring to a simmer over medium heat, add black pepper, onion, and shrimp, stir and simmer for 8-10 minutes.
2. Add dill, stir, cook for 5 minutes more, ladle into bowls and serve.
3. Enjoy!

 NUTRITION

Calories: 190 Protein: 8 g Fat: 7 g Carbs: 12 g

Pork and Lentil Soup

 6 servings 70 minutes

 ## DIRECTIONS

1. Heat a saucepan with the oil over medium heat, add garlic, onion, basil, ginger, salt, pepper and cumin, stir well and cook for 6 minutes.
2. Add carrots, stir and cook 5 more minutes. Add pork and brown for a few minutes.
3. Add lentils, tomato paste and stock, stir, bring to a boil, cover pan and simmer for 50 minutes.
4. Transfer pork to a plate, discard bones, shred it and return to pan.
5. Add chili flakes and lime juice, stir, ladle into bowls and serve.

 ## INGREDIENTS

1 small yellow onion, chopped

1 tablespoon olive oil

1 and ½ teaspoons basil, chopped

1 and ½ teaspoons ginger, grated

3 garlic cloves, chopped

Salt and black pepper to taste

½ teaspoon cumin, ground

1 carrot, chopped

1 pound pork chops, bone-in 3 ounces brown lentils, rinsed

3 cups chicken stock

2 tablespoons tomato paste

2 tablespoons lime juice

1 teaspoon red chili flakes, crushed

 ## NUTRITION

Calories: 263 Protein: 10 g Fat: 4 g Carbs: 8 g

Mediterranean Ground Beef Soup

 8 servings   40 minutes

 INGREDIENTS

1 yellow onion, chopped
1 tablespoon olive oil
1 garlic clove, minced
1 pound beef, ground
1 pound eggplant, chopped
¾ cup celery, chopped
¾ cup carrots, chopped
Salt and black pepper to taste
29 ounces canned tomatoes, drained and chopped
28 ounces beef stock
½ teaspoon nutmeg, ground
½ cup macaroni
2 teaspoons parsley, chopped
½ cup parmesan cheese, grated

DIRECTIONS

1. Heat a large saucepan with the oil over medium heat, add onion, garlic, and meat, stir and brown for a few minutes.
2. Add celery, carrots, eggplant, and tomatoes and stir.
3. Add stock, salt, pepper, and nutmeg.
4. Stir and cook for 20 minutes. Add macaroni, stir and cook for 12 minutes.
5. Ladle into soup bowls, top with grated cheese and serve.

 NUTRITION

Calories: 241 Protein: 10 g Fat: 3 g Carbs: 7 g

Beef and Lentil Soup

 8 servings   1 h 50 min

 ## INGREDIENTS

1 pound beef chuck, cubed

2 tablespoons olive oil

2 celery stalks, chopped

2 carrots, chopped

1 yellow onion, chopped

Salt and black pepper to taste

3 garlic cloves, chopped

2 cups lentils

32 ounces canned chicken stock

1 ½ teaspoons cilantro, dried

1 teaspoon oregano, dried

28 ounces canned tomatoes, chopped

¼ cup parsley, chopped

½ cup parmesan, grated

 ## DIRECTIONS

1. Heat a saucepan with the oil over medium-high heat, add beef, salt, and pepper to taste, stir, brown for 8 minutes, transfer to a plate and keep warm.

2. Return saucepan to medium heat, add carrots, celery, garlic, onion, oregano, and cilantro, stir and cook for 8 more minutes.

3. Return beef to saucepan and also add stock and tomatoes, stir, bring to a boil, cover pan and cook for 1 hour.

4. Add lentils, stir and simmer for 40 more minutes.

5. Add salt, pepper to taste, parsley, stir, ladle into bowls, sprinkle parmesan on top and serve.

 ## NUTRITION

Calories: 210 Protein: 10 g Fat: 4 g Carbs: 8 g

Italian Egg-drop Soup

 6 servings   🕐 68minutes

 **INGREDIENTS**

2 big eggs

4 big egg white

1 teaspoon of olive oil

1 medium of shallot

8 cups of chicken stock

1 bay leaf

1 tablespoon of salt

½ tablespoon of pepper

¼ cup of parmesan cheese (cheese)

6 cloves of garlic

½ cup of chopped parsley

2 tablespoons of thyme leaves

1 big onion

 DIRECTIONS

1. Add oil into a big pot and let it heat for about 30 seconds.

2. Put onion, garlic, shallot, let it cook for 3 minutes Put the parsley, thyme, stock, and bay leaf. Set timer for 45minutes.

3. Include spinach and let it stay for 5 minutes Put egg, egg white in a bowl and whisk.

4. Mix the eggs well and let it cook for about 5 minutes.

5. Add pepper, salt. Put grated parmesan on top by sprinkling

6. It is ready to be served.

 NUTRITION

Calories: 53.7kcal Carbs: 1.4g Fat: 3.4g Protein: 4.7g

Chapter 7:
DESSERT

Peach Sorbet

 4 servings    15 minutes

INGREDIENTS

4 medium peaches, sliced (approx. 3 1/2 cups)

1 tbsp raw honey

1 tsp lemon juice

1/4 cup warm water, as needed

 DIRECTIONS

11. Slice the ripe peaches and remove the pit.

2. Lay out the fresh peach slices over a rimmed baking sheet lined with parchment paper.

3. Freeze the peach slices until completely solid, which should take at least 3-4 hours, or overnight.

4. Place the frozen peach slices into the bowl of a food processor or heavy duty blender, along with a little raw honey, and freshly squeezed lemon juice.

5. Blend until smooth.

6. You may need to add a little warm water and press down with a spatula to help the process along.

7. Eat immediately for a softer texture, or transfer into a freezer-safe container and freeze for 3-4 hours or until firm.

 NUTRITION

calories 70kcal ;protein 1g ;carbs 17g ; fiber 2g

Cranberry Pear Pie

 8 servings    70 minutes

 ## INGREDIENTS

Pastry for single-crust pie (9 inches)

2 tablespoons all-purpose flour

1/2 cup maple syrup

2 tablespoons butter, melted

5 cups sliced peeled fresh pears

1 cup fresh or frozen cranberries

Topping:

1/2 cup all-purpose flour

1/4 cup packed brown sugar

1 teaspoon ground cinnamon

1/3 cup cold butter, cubed

1/2 cup chopped walnuts

 ## DIRECTIONS

1. Line a 9-in. pie plate with pastry; trim and flute edges. Set aside.

2. In a large bowl, combine the flour, syrup and butter until smooth.

3. Add pears and cranberries; toss to coat. Spoon into crust.

4. For topping, combine the flour, brown sugar and cinnamon; cut in butter until crumbly.

5. Stir in walnuts. Sprinkle over filling.

6. Cover edges of crust loosely with foil to prevent overbrowning.

7. Bake at 400° for 15 minutes. Reduce heat to 350°.

8. Remove foil; bake 35-40 minutes longer or until crust is golden brown and filling is bubbly.

9. Cool on a wire rack.

 ## NUTRITION

calories 483kcal ;protein 5g ;carbs 59g ; fat 27g ; fiber 5g

Lemon Cream

  2 servings   30 minutes

 INGREDIENTS

155g (2/3 cup) lemon juice

zest of 2 lemons

165 g (3/4 cup) granulated
sugar

100 g (2 large) eggs

40 g (2 large) egg yolks

pinch of salt

226 g (8 oz) unsalted
butter, diced and
at room temperature

 NUTRITION

calories 188kcal ;protein 1g ;carbs 27g ;
fat 8g

 DIRECTIONS

1. Place the lemon juice, zest, sugar, eggs, egg yolks, and salt into a medium heatproof bowl

2. set over a small saucepan filled with an inch of simmering water.

3. Whisk constantly until the mixture thickens, about 10 minutes.

4. The temperature should read 170°F/75°C, and the mixture should coat the back of a wooden spoon.

5. Pour through a fine sieve into a blender.

6. Allow the cream to cool for about 15 minutes (the temperature should be approximately 140°F/60°C).

7. Blend the butter into the lemon mixture, a couple of pieces at a time.

8. Once all the butter has been added and incorporated, pour the lemon filling into a container.

9. Place a sheet of plastic wrap directly onto the surface of the filling to prevent a 'skin' from forming.

10. Refrigerate for at least 4 hours before enjoying.

Apple & Blueberry Stew

 5 servings   8 minutes

 INGREDIENTS

1 medium apple, peeled, cored and
chopped
60g frozen blueberries
150ml water

 DIRECTIONS

1. Put the chopped apple and blueberries
into a saucepan, add 150ml water.
2. Cook for around 10 minutes until the
apple and blueberry are completely soft.
3. If it sticks to the pan, add a little more
water.
4. Pour the mixture into a bowl and stir.
5. Cool down and then serve.

 NUTRITION

calories 190kcal

Mandarin Cream

  16 servings   17 minutes

 ## INGREDIENTS

Crust:

9 tablespoons butter or stick margarine, softened

½ cup sugar

1 teaspoon vanilla extrac

1 ½ cups all-purpose flour

⅛ teaspoon salt

Cooking spray

Filling:

2 (11-ounce) cans mandarin oranges in light syrup, undrained

¼ cup sugar

1 (16-ounce) carton fat-free sour cream

1 (8-ounce) carton low-fat sour cream

2 (3.4-ounce) packages vanilla instant pudding mix or 2 (1.4-ounce) packages sugar-free vanilla instant pudding mix

1 (8-ounce) container frozen reduced-calorie whipped topping, thawed

Mint sprigs (optional)

 ## NUTRITION

calories 276kcal ;carbs 43g ; fat 9g

DIRECTIONS

1. To prepare crust, combine the butter, 1/2 cup sugar, and vanilla in a large bowl.

2. Beat at medium speed of a mixer until light and fluffy (about 2 minutes).

3. Lightly spoon flour into dry measuring cups; level with a knife.

4. Add flour and salt to butter mixture, beating at low speed until well blended.

5. Preheat oven to 400°.

6. Pat dough into a 13 x 9-inch baking dish coated with cooking spray, and pierce bottom of dough with a fork.

7. Bake at 400° for 12 minutes or until lightly browned.

8. Cool crust on a wire rack.

9. To prepare filling, drain mandarin oranges over a large bowl, reserving 1/2 cup juice.

10. Combine juice, 1/4 cup sugar, sour creams, and pudding mix in a large bowl.

11. Stir in the orange segments.

12. Spoon orange mixture over crust, spreading evenly. Top with whipped topping.

13. Chill 1 hour. Garnish with mint, if desired.

Strawberries With Mint Whipped Cream

 4 servings   20 minutes

 INGREDIENTS

1/4 cup sugar

2 packed cups fresh mint leaves and
stems, coarsely chopped, plus sprigs for
garnish

1 cup heavy cream

1 quart strawberries, hulled and thinly
sliced

 **DIRECTIONS**

1. Make syrup: In a medium saucepan over medium
heat, bring sugar, mint, and 2 tablespoons water to a
boil.

2. Remove from heat; steep 15 minutes.

3. Strain through a finemesh sieve into a measuring
cup, pressing to extract as much liquid as possible.

4. Discard solids. Let cool (makes about 1/4 cup).

5. Meanwhile, in a large bowl, whip cream until stiff
peaks form.

6. Gently fold in 1/4 cup syrup (store any remaining
syrup); if needed, re-whip cream to stiffen.

7. Starting with strawberries, spoon alternating
layers of strawberries and cream into four serving
glasses.

8. Top each with a mint sprig.

 NUTRITION

calories 230kcal

Vanilla Cake

 14 servings 45 minutes

 ## DIRECTIONS

1. Preheat oven to 350°F. Butter and flour two 9" cake pans, tapping out excess flour.
2. In a medium bowl, whisk together flour, baking powder and salt. Set flour mixture aside.
3. In a large mixing bowl using an electric hand mixer (or stand mixer), beat butter and sugar on medium-high speed for 5 minutes until thick and fluffy, scraping down the bowl as needed.
4. Add 4 eggs, one at a time, beating well with each addition then scrape down the bowl.
5. Add 4 tsp vanilla extract and beat to combine.
6. Reduce mixer to medium speed and add the flour mixture in thirds alternating with the 1 cup of room temperature buttermilk, allowing the flour and buttermilk to incorporate with each addition.
7. Scrape down the bowl as needed and beat until just combined and smooth.
8. Divide batter evenly between 2 prepared cake pans and spread out the batter into the pans smoothing out the tops with a spatula.
9. Bake on the center rack at 350°F for 28-30 minutes.
10. Rest in pans for 10 minutes then run a knife or thin spatula around the edges to loosen and turn out onto a wire rack to cool completely before applying Vanilla Frosting.

 ## INGREDIENTS

2 1/2 cups all-purpose flour

1 Tbsp baking powder

1/2 tsp fine salt

1 cup unsalted butter, softened

1 1/2 cups granulated sugar

4 large eggs, room temperature

4 tsp pure vanilla extract

1 cup buttermilk, or plain kefir, room temperature

 ## NUTRITION

calories 313kcal ;protein 5g ;carbs 40g ; fat 1g ; fiber 15g

Berry Smoothie Bowl

🍴 2 servings   🕐 29 minutes

 INGREDIENTS

½ cup strawberry (75 g)

½ cup raspberry (60 g)

1 cup blackberry (55 g)

1 banana, sliced

½ cup greek yogurt (140 g)

¼ cup almond milk (60 mL), or soy milk

¼ cup peanut butter (60 g)

DIRECTIONS

1. Add the berries, banana, Greek yogurt, almond milk, and peanut butter to a blender and blend until smooth.
2. Top with your favorite toppings.

NUTRITION

Calories: 1709 Fat: 130 grams Carbs: 108 grams Fiber: 37 grams Sugars: 48 grams Protein: 57 grams

Coconut Mint Ice Cream

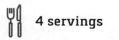 4 servings   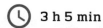 3 h 5 min

 ## DIRECTIONS

1. Place the freezer bowl of your ice cream maker into the freezer the day before you
2. plan to make ice cream.
3. Scoop the chilled coconut cream from the cans, leave out the liquid.
4. Remove the pit and peel from the avocado.
5. In a food process place the coconut cream, avocado, raw honey and peppermint extract in a bowl of a food processor, blend until smooth.
6. Transfer coconut milk mixture to an ice cream maker bowl, follow the instructions on your ice cream maker and churn until the ice cream is thick and smooth.
7. With the mixer still running, add in the chocolate chips and process until just combined.
8. Once the ice cream is firm, remove from the ice cream maker and place in a freezer-safe bowl or container.
9. Freeze for at least 3 hours to allow the ice cream to harden.
10. Before serving, allow ice cream to sit out at room temperature for 5-10 minutes until it's soft enough to scoop.

 ## INGREDIENTS

2 cans full fat coconut milk, chilled
1/3 cup raw honey
1 whole avocado
1 teaspoon peppermint extract
3/4 cup chocolate chips

 ## NUTRITION

calories 595kcal ;protein 5g
;carbs 37g ; fat 50g ; fiber 4g

Chocolate Cherry Cream

🍴 15 servings   🕐 4 h 25 min

INGREDIENTS

1 cup semi-sweet chocolate chips

1/3 cup evaporated milk

1/2 cups sifted powdered sugar

1/3 cup chopped nuts

1/3 cup chopped maraschino cherry, well drained

1/4 cups coconut or 1 1/4 cups chopped nuts

DIRECTIONS

1. Melt chocolate and milk over low heat.
2. Remove from heat.
3. Stir in powdered sugar, nuts and cherries, mix well.
4. Chill until cool enough to handle.
5. Shape into 1-inch balls and roll in nuts or coconut.
6. Chill at least 4 hours.

NUTRITION

calories 108kcal ;protein 1g ;carbs 13g ; fat 6g ; fiber 1g

Conclusion

Congratulations on completing your journey through "The Mediterranean Diet Cookbook for Beginners 2024"! Over the course of this culinary adventure, you've explored 2000 days' worth of simple yet mouthwatering Mediterranean diet recipes, each designed to tantalize your taste buds while promoting health and wellness.

As you've discovered, the Mediterranean diet isn't just about what you eat—it's a lifestyle that celebrates fresh, whole foods, vibrant flavors, and the joy of sharing meals with loved ones. By embracing this way of eating, you've not only nourished your body but also cultivated a deeper appreciation for the rich culinary traditions of the Mediterranean region.

Throughout this cookbook, you've been treated to a visual feast, with full-color pictures accompanying each recipe, inspiring you to get creative in the kitchen. And with easy-to-find ingredients, you've been able to whip up delicious meals without any hassle, making the Mediterranean diet accessible to beginners and seasoned cooks alike.

But your journey doesn't end here. Armed with the knowledge and skills you've gained, you're now equipped to continue exploring the endless possibilities of Mediterranean cuisine. Whether you're looking to maintain a healthy lifestyle, impress guests with your culinary prowess, or simply savor the flavors of the Mediterranean, this cookbook will be your trusted companion on your gastronomic adventures.

So here's to you, and here's to the vibrant, flavorful world of the Mediterranean diet. May your culinary journey be filled with delicious discoveries, memorable meals, and moments shared around the table. Bon appétit!

Thank You

Dear Esteemed Reader:

You're just one step away from getting a copy of our work along with some really cool gifts and the latest updates. All you need to do is either visit the link or scan the QR code below, or drop us an email.

Or is it a particular part of our work tiptoe into your heart, or did a wee error play hide-and-seek amidst our pages? We believe your perspective is our lighthouse, guiding us gradually towards refinement.

We invite you to convey your thoughts or hiccuped observations through whichever of our dedicated channels suits your style. Your voice is precious to us, a melody we are eagerly awaiting.

https://forms.gle/2RDDh5SnhWQwTLuP7

Author's email: laihongchun70@gmail.com

Best regards,

Carol Kelley

Carol Kelley

22095598R00051